TENSES : THE BLOSSOMS OF ENGLISH GRAMMAR

ANKITA SINGH

The book is dedicated to all English learners .

The book is dedicated to Shri M.L . Singh Yadav my maternal
grandfather who from childhood inspired me a lot to learn English
tenses considered as foundation of English Grammar .

Contents

Acknowledgements

It is my immense pleasure to acknowledge Almighty God, who gave me inspiration to write on English tenses. I'am heartly thankful to my parents Mrs. Madhu Yadav and Mr. Hemant Kumar their guidance at each moment of life provide me a platform to climb ladder of success. Further I'am thankful to publishers to bring my manuscript in book form.

-Ankita Singh

CHAPTER ONE

TENSES: INTRODUCTION

- *Students will understand the concept of time and action.*
- *Students will able acknowledge basic rules regarding tenses.*
- *Students will able to learn and identify different forms of verb mandatory to understand tenses.*
- *Students will able to understand the concept of helping verbs.*
- *Students will learn about different types of tenses.*

INTRODUCTION TO TENSES

In English Grammar tenses are backbone of any sentence structure. It represents time and action. Tense illustrates action of verb or its state of being, such as present (something that is happening now), past (something that happened earlier), future (something predicted to happen in future).

KEY TERMINOLOGY TO REMEMBER IN TENSES

TIME: It is crucial element in tense. Tense denotes a certain time at which particular course of action is been performed.

ACTION ——▶VERB

Action : It represents verb.

TYPES OF TENSES

In broad terms tenses are of three kinds – Past , Present , Future , which is further subdivided into four major parts illustrated in figure 1.1

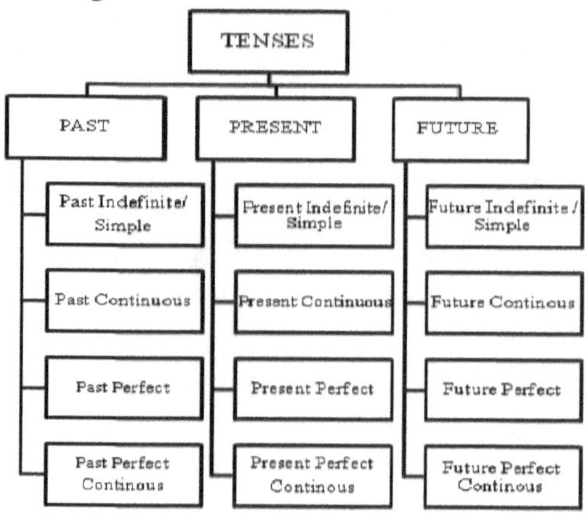

Figure 1.1 Types of Tenses

PAST TENSE

- Past Indefinite
- Past Continuous
- Past Perfect
- Past Perfect Continuous

PRESENT TENSE

- Present Indefinite
- Present Continuous

- Present Perfect
- Present Perfect continuous

FUTURE TENSE

- Future Indefinite
- Future Continuous
- Future Perfect
- Future perfect Continuous

Hence, there are total 12 tenses in English Grammar.

Prior to study tenses in depth, let's have a look on forms of verbs which are mandatory in context of learning tenses.

FORMS OF VERB

VERB FIRST FORM: The First form of verb is used with Present indefinite tense.

Illustrations: Sing, Play, eat, take, read, write, paint etc.

VERB SECOND FORM: Second form of verb is used with past Indefinite tense.

Illustrations: Played, ate, took, read, wrote, painted etc.

VERB THIRD FORM: Third form of verb is used with perfect tense of all tenses i.e. "Past perfect tense, Present perfect tense, Future perfect tense". Here mostly the word ends with "ed or n".

Illustration: Played, taken, beaten, eaten etc.

VERB 1ST FORM PLUS +ING: It is used with Continuous tense including present continuous tense, past continuous tense, future continuous tense.

Illustrations

1. singing [sing denotes verb First form + Ing = singing]
2. Reading [Read denotes verb First form + Ing = Reading]

3. Dancing [Dance denotes verb First form +Ing = Dancing]
4. Walking [walk denotes verb First form+Ing = walking]
5. Climbing [climb denotes verb First form + Ing = climbing]

CONCEPTS OF HELPING VERB

Helping verbs are also known as auxiliary verbs, these are meant to support other verbs.

Do

Be – is/am/ are/ was / were / being / been / will be.

Have – Has / have / had/ having / will have

SOME COMMON HELPING VERB

Am , is, are , was , were , being , been , and , be , have , has , had , do ,does , did , will , would , shall , should.

IDENTIFICATION OF TENSES THROUGH HELPING VERB AND FORM OF MAIN VERBS

TENSE	INDEFINITE	CONTINUOUS	PERFECT	PERFECT CONTINUOUS
PRESENT	Helping verb " Do/Does" Main Verb Ist Form Example: play , sing	Helping verb Is/ am / Are MV Ist form + ing Example is singing	Helping verb Has/ Have Main verb III form Example : has taken	Helping verb Has/ Have Been MV Ist form +ing
PAST	Helping verb " Did" Main verb II Form Example : ate	Helping verb was/ were MV Ist form +ing Example: was singing	Helping Verb Had Main Verb III form Example : Had taken	Helping verb Had Been MV Ist form +ing
FUTURE	Helping verb will/shall Main verb I form Example: will play	Helping verb will be /shall be MV Ist form +ing	Helping verb Have Main verb III form Example : Have taken	Helping verb Have Been MV Ist form +ing

Figure 1.2 Tenses identification through helping verbs and forms of main verbs.

** Note the important points:

a. "Do" is used with plural .
b. "Does" is used with singular.
c. "Is" is used with singular .
d. "Are" is used with plural .
e. "Am" is used with I.
f. "Was" is used with singular.
g. "Were" is used with plural.
h. "Will" is used with singular.
a. "Shall" is used with plural.

EVALUATION
EXPLAIN

1. Parts of tenses
2. Present continuous tense
3. Forms of Main verb
4. Auxiliary verbs

ONE WORD QUERY

1. Main verb I form + ing is used in which kind of tense ....
2. Main verb III form is used in which tense......................
3. Second form of verb is used with ....
4. Radha is dancing is denotes what? ....
5. Do is used with ....

CHAPTER TWO

PRESENT INDEFINITE TENSE

OBJECTIVES OF STUDY

- *Students will learn concept of present indefinite tense.*
- *Students will acknowledge techniques to identify present Indefinite tense.*
- *Students will make keynotes regarding structure of present indefinite tense.*
- *Students will able to construct sentences using present indefinite tense.*

KEY POINTS OF PRESENT INDEFINITE TENSE

Habitual action: Present indefinite or simple present tense is used to express habitual actions.

Examples

1. Mohan eats cornflakes every morning.
2. Radha drinks tea every morning.
3. My father read newspaper every morning.
4. I get up every day at four o' clock

Universal truth: Present indefinite tense is used to express general or universal truths.

Examples

1. The sun rises in the east.
2. Mango is a fruit.
3. The Ganga is a holy river.

Expression of future event that is part of fixed schedule: Present indefinite tense is used to express future event that is part of fixed time table or programme. It can be better illustrated through examples mentioned below:

1. The flight leaves at 5.30
2. The movie starts at 9o' clock.
3. The next bus is at 8.00 tomorrow morning.

Quotations: Further the simple present tense is also used to express quotations.

Example

John keats says, 'Beauty is truth, truth beauty'

STRUCTURE OF PRESENT INDEFINITE TENSE

To understand present indefinite tense thoroughly let's have a look on structure of present indefinite or simple present tense.

RULE IN CASE OF AFFIRMATIVE SENTENCE

Subject + main verb first form + es /s + object

Illustrations:

• Aryan plays golf.

Let's break the sentence to access its parts -
subject = Aryan

Main verb first form= play
es/s= s
object = golf
Hence, sentence becomes Aryan plays golf.

- The moon shines in the sky.

  Subject= The moon
  Main verb first form = shine
  es/s = s
  object = sky

- Rohan eats mango.

  subject = Rohan
  Main verb first form= eat
  es/s= s
  Object = Mango
  SOME MORE EXAMPLES

1. I write articles on current topics.
2. I love to listen old songs.
3. He loves to travel around the globe.
4. He sings a song .
5. The Sun sets in west.
6. She prefers milk to cornflakes.
7. She goes to gym everyday.
8. Here comes the aircraft!
9. He does yoga every morning.
10. The train leaves at 6:30 PM.

RULE IN CASE OF NEGATIVE SENTENCE
Subject +do/ does+ not + main verb first form + object

Note Does is used with singular , do is used with plural"

Illustrations :

- Radha does not like grapes.

  subject= Radha
  Do/does= does
  Not = not
  Main verb first form= like
  object= grapes

- Dogs do not eat sweets.

  Subject= Dogs
  Do/does= do
  Not= not
  Main verb first form= eat
  Object= sweets

- Sumit does not know English.

  Subject = sumit
  Do/does = does
  Not= not
  Main verb first from= know
  Object= English

- I do not like coffee.

  Subject= I
  Do/does= do
  Not= not
  Main verb first form = like

Object= coffee.
SOME MORE EXAMPLES

1. I do not go to gym.
2. Ram does not know time.
3. Arvind does not grow crops.
4. Radha does not browse internet.
5. She does not play pub g .
6. They do not debate in public.
7. I do not know German.
8. Sita does not eat mango.
9. She does not know the art of cooking.
10. They do not like rabbit.

RULE IN CASE OF INTERROGATIVE SENTENCES
Do/Does + subject +main verb first form + object ?
Illustration :

- Does she likes tea?

  Do/Does= Does
  Subject= she
  Main verb first form = likes
  Object= tea ?

- Do you know German language?

  Do/Does= Do
  Subject= you
  Main verb first form = know
  Object= German language
  SOME MORE EXAMPLES

1. Does he develop android apps?
2. Does he use social media ?
3. Do you know English grammar?
4. Does Radha likes coffee?
5. Does farmer grow crops?
6. Does dog sleeps on cozy bed?
7. Do they sell mobile cover?
8. Do they play pub g?
9. Does Ram lives in Ayodhya?
10. Do you like burger?

RULE IN CASE OF DOUBLE INTERROGATIVE SENTENCES

WH family + Do/does +subject +main verb first form + object

Note – "WH family" includes-
Who
What
Where
When
Why
Which
How
Illustration

• How do you know him ?

WH family = How
Do/does= do
Subject= you
Main verb first form = know
Object= him
SOME MORE EXAMPLE

1. Where do they live?
2. Why does he use social media?
3. Why do you like burger?
4. How do you know me?
5. Why do they play pub g?
6. Why do they sell mobile cover?
7. Why does Radha eat ice cream?
8. Why do they ride bicycle?
9. What does your brother do ?
10. What does your mother bake in the microwave ?

EVALUATION

1. Make ten sentences using present indefinite tense.

1. Find out affirmative, negative, interrogative, double interrogative sentences from mix examples of present indefinite tense .

a. I write a letter.
b. She does hard work.
c. Ashman runs very fast.
d. He does not work hard.
e. We do not sleep in the courtyard.
f. They do not fight with their brothers.
g. Does Nishant go to school daily ?
h. Where do you live ?
i. Does your grandfather love you ?

CHAPTER THREE

PRESENT CONTINUOUS TENSE

OBJECTIVES OF STUDY

- *Students will learn the concept and rule of present continuous tense.*
- *Students will able to identify present continuous tense in sentences.*
- *Students will learn the form of verb used in present continuous tense.*
- *Students will make keynotes regarding structure of present continuous tense.*
- *Students will able to construct sentences using present continuous tense.*

KEY POINTS TO REMEMBER IN PRESENT CONTINUOUS TENSE

Present continuous tense is also called present progressive tense. It denotes action which is happening now and may continue into future.

It is mandatory to acknowledge that main verb first form + ing is key element in construction of sentences related to present continuous tense.

STRUCTURE OF PRESENT CONTINUOUS TENSE

To understand present continuous tense in detail its essential to study structure of present continuous tense .

RULE IN CASE OF AFFIRMATIVE SENTENCE

Subject + is/ am/ are+ main verb first form + ing + object

Note : * " IS" is used with singular , am is used with "I" , and " ARE" is used with plural.

Illustration

- Kajal is doing Yoga.

  Subject = Kajal
  is/am/are = is
  Main verb first form= do
  +
  ing
  object = yoga

- Dog is eating calcium.

  Subject = Dog
  is/am/are = is
  Main verb first form= eat
  +
  ing
  object = calcium

- Radha is writing letter.

  Subject = Radha
  is/am/are = is
  Main verb first form= write

+

ing

object = letter

- They are playing cricket .

  Subject = They
  is/am/are = are
  Main verb first form= play
  +
  ing
  object = cricket

- I am watching movie.

  Subject = I
  is/am/are = am
  Main verb first form= watch
  +
  ing
  object = movie

  SOME MORE EXAMPLES

1. Shyam is playing flute.
2. Tammana is eating popcorn.
3. Doves are swimming in pool.
4. They are fighting for pencil.
5. Daisy is knitting cap.
6. Raghav is doing homework.
7. Gaurav is watching T.V.
8. Mr. Arnav is attending conference.
9. Anu is drinking coffee.
10. I am listening old commentaries.

Note : * In Present continuous tense we always use " Main verb first form + ing .

Example – Learn (Main verb 1ˢᵗ form) + ing ______ Learning.

Sing (Main verb 1ˢᵗ form) + ing _____ singing.

Dance (Main verb 1ˢᵗ form) + ing _____ Dancing.

Fight(Main verb 1ˢᵗ form) + ing ______ Fighting

RULE IN CASE OF NEGATIVE SENTENCES

Subject + is/ am / are + not + main verb first form + ing + object

- She is not reading Newspaper.

  Subject= she
  is/am/ are= is
  not
  Main verb first form = read
  +
  ing
  Object= newspaper

- He is not doing painting.

  Subject= He
  is/am/ are= is
  not
  Main verb first form = do
  +
  ing
  Object= painting

- They are not playing cricket.

Subject= They
is/am/ are= are
not
Main verb first form = play
+
ing
Object= cricket

• Raman is not learning english

Subject= Raman
is/am/ are= is
not
Main verb first form = learn
+
ing
Object= English

SOME MORE EXAMPLES

1. Tammana is not eating popcorn.
2. Doves are not swimming in pool.
3. They are not fighting for pencil.
4. Daisy is not knitting cap.
5. Raghav is not doing homework.
6. Gaurav is not watching T.V.
7. Mr. Arnav is not attending conference.
8. Anurag is not drinking coffee.
9. I am not listening old commentaries.
10. They are not going to Mumbai.

RULE IN CASE OF INTERROGATIVE SENTENCE
Is /am/ are + subject + main verb first form + ing + object

- Are they going to New Delhi ?

  Is/ am / are = Are
  Subject= they
  Main verb first form= go
  +
  ing
  Object= New Delhi

- Is She Playing foot ball?

  Is/ am / are = Is
  Subject= she
  Main verb first form= play
  +
  ing
  Object= football

- Am I surfing internet?

  Is/ am / are = Am
  Subject= I
  Main verb first form= surf
  +
  ing
  Object= internet

- Is she writing letter?

  Is/ am / are = Is
  Subject= she
  Main verb first form= write
  +

ing
Object= letter

- Is dog sleeping outside?

Is/ am / are = Is
Subject= dog
Main verb first form= sleep
+
ing
Object= outside

SOME MORE EXAMPLES

1. Are they baking cake?
2. Is she going to school?
3. Is tiger playing with cubs?
4. Are boys playing chess?
5. Are you dancing on floor?
6. Is kamal taking tea?
7. Are they walking in the park?
8. Is Zoo administration bringing new zebra?
9. Is she painting daffodils ?
10. Are they making squash ?

RULE IN CASE OF DOUBLE INTERROGATIVE SENTENCE

WH family +Is /am are + subject + main verb first form + ing + object

Note – "WH family" includes-

Who

What

Where

When

Why
Which
How

- Where are you going today ?

  WH family= where
  Helping verb Is/ am / are = are
  Subject= you
  Main verb first form = go
  +
  ing
  Object= today

- Why is she watching T.V. ?

  WH family= Why
  Helping verb Is/ am/ are = is
  Subject= She
  Main verb first form= watch
  +
  ing
  Object= T.V

- What is she doing upstairs ?

  WH family = what
  Helping verb Is/ am/ are= is
  Subject= she
  Main verb first form = do
  +
  ing
  Object= upstairs

- Why is she painting daffodils ?

WH family= why
Helping verb Is/ am / are = is
Subject= she
Main verb first form = paint
+

ing
Object= daffodils
SOME MORE EXAMPLES

1. Why are they baking cake?
2. When is she going to Mumbai ?
3. Where is tiger playing with cubs?
4. Why are boys playing chess?
5. Why are you dancing on floor?
6. What is she doing with T.V remote ?
7. How is he going to village ?
8. Where is she going today ?
9. Why is she eating toffee .
10. Why is Radha fighting with Ramesh ?

EVALUATION

1. Construct ten sentences using present continuous tense.

1. Find out affirmative, negative, interrogative, double interrogative sentences from mix examples of present continuous tense .

a. Shyam is playing flute.
b. Doves are swimming in pool.
c. Ducks are not swimming in river.

d. Manoj is not throwing garbage .
e. Is Mohan writing letter?
f. Is Ashman playing video game?
g. Am I going to grandfather's house?
h. Why is she painting landscape?
i. Why is he eating medicine?

CHAPTER FOUR

PRESENT PERFECT TENSE

OBJECTIVES OF STUDY

- *Students will understand the concept of present perfect tense.*
- *Students will learn the rules related to present perfect tense.*
- *Students will able to identify present perfect tense in sentence.*
- *Students will learn the form of verb used in present perfect tense.*
- *Students will make keynotes regarding structure of present perfect tense.*
- *Students will able to construct sentences using present perfect tense.*

KEY POINTS TO REMEMBER IN PRESENT PERFECT TENSE

Present perfect tense denotes action which was occurred at indefinite time in past and still continued to present time.

It is essential to acknowledge that in main verb third form is key element in construction of sentences related to present perfect tense.

RULE IN CASE OF AFFIRMATIVE SENTENCE

To understand present perfect tense in detail its essential to study structure of present perfect tense .

Subject + has/ have + main verb third form +object.

Note* - Has is used with singular.

Have is used with plural.

- I have taken medicine .

  Subject= I
  Has/ have = have
  Main verb third form = taken
  Object = medicine

- He has eaten my cake.

  Subject= He
  Has/ have = has
  Main verb third form = eaten
  Object = my cake

- They have bought a red car.

  Subject= They
  Has/ have = have
  Main verb third form = bought
  Object = red car

- We have met him.

  Subject= we
  Has/ have = have

Main verb third form = met
Object = him

• Raman has beaten my puppy .

Subject= Raman
Has/ have = has
Main verb third form = beaten
Object = my puppy
SOME MORE EXAMPLE

1. She has forgotten her bag.
2. He has taken my pencil.
3. He has finished his manuscript.
4. She has lost her wedding ring.
5. He has broken his left hand.
6. Rohan has started new job.
7. Diksha has forgotten English tenses.
8. We have met him.
9. I have seen blue birds.
10. He has reached London.

RULE IN CASE OF NEGATIVE SENTENCE
Subject + has / have + not+ main verb third form + object
Illustration

• I have not seen blue birds.

Subject= I
Has / have= have
Not = not
Main verb third form = seen

Object = blue birds

- He has not reached office.

  Subject = He
  Has / have = has
  Not = not
  Main verb third form = reached
  Object = office

- Diksha has not eaten Mango.

  Subject = Diksha
  Has / have = has
  Not = not
  Main verb third form = eaten
  Object = Mango

- He has not taken my pencil.

  Subject = He
  Has / have = has
  Not = not
  Main verb third form = taken
  Object = my pencil

- We have not met him.

  Subject = we
  Has / have = have
  Not = not
  Main verb third form = met
  Object = him

SOME MORE EXAMPLES

1. She has not forgotten her bag.
2. He has not taken my book.
3. He has not finished his manuscript.
4. She has not lost her wedding ring.
5. He has not broken his leg.
6. Rohan has not started a new job.
7. Ram has not forgotten my name.
8. We have not met him.
9. I have not seen blue birds.
10. He has not reached home.

RULE IN CASE OF INTERROGATIVE SENTENCE
Has/ have + subject + main verb third form + object

- Have you won the football match ?

  Has / have = Have
  Subject= you
  Main verb third form= won
  Object = foot ball match ?

- Have you written assignments ?

  Has / have = Have
  Subject= you
  Main verb third form= written
  Object= Assignment ?

- Have you seen blue birds?

  Has/ have = Have

subject = you
Main verb third form = seen
object = blue birds

- Has she written manuscript?

  Has / have = Has
  Subject= she
  Main verb third form= written
  Object= manuscript?

- Has he beaten my puppy ?

  Has / have = Has
  subject = he
  Main verb third form = beaten
  object= my puppy
  SOME MORE EXAMPLES

1. Have they ever played pub g?
2. Has Anant missed the bus ?
3. Has she visited U.K?
4. Has he sent you letter?
5. Have you ever seen Tiger ?
6. Have they taken camel ride?
7. Have you done your homework ?
8. Have they met Professor Shaw?
9. Has she taken medicine?
10. Has Ram learnt Psychology ?

RULE IN CASE OF DOUBLE INTERROGATIVE SENTENCE

WH Family + has / have + subject + main verb third form + object

Note * WH Family includes:

Who

What

Where

When

Why

Which

How

Who

What

Where

When

Why

Which

How

Illustration:

- When have you won the trophy?

  WH family = when
  Has/ have = have
  Subject = you
  Main verb third form = won
  Object = the trophy

- How have you done the homework?

  WH family = How
  Has/ have = have
  Subject = you
  Main verb third form = done

Object = the homework

- Where have you met Mr. Brown Nicolas ?

  WH family = where
  Has/ have= have
  Subject= you
  Main verb third form = met
  Object = Mr. Brown Nicolas

- Where have you seen blue birds?

  WH family = where
  Has/ have= have
  Subject= you
  Main verb third form = seen
  Object = blue birds

SOME MORE EXAMPLES

1. Why has she not came home?
2. Why has she not taken bed rest?
3. where have you seen white tiger?
4. How have you done your assignment ?
5. Why has she beaten your pet ?
6. Why has she taken your notebook ?
7. Where have they went yesterday ?
8. How have they managed the tight budget ?
9. when have they developed android app ?
10. where have you watched the drama?

EVALUATION

1. Write ten sentence related to present perfect tense

1. One word query

a. which form of verb is used in present perfect tense............
b. write affirmative sentence structure in context of present perfect tense.......
c. Write negative sentence structure in context of present perfect tense......

CHAPTER FIVE

PRESENT PERFECT CONTINUOUS TENSE

OBJECTIVES OF STUDY

- *Students will understand the concept of present perfect continuous tense.*
- *Students will acknowledge rules to construct sentences related to present perfect continuous tense.*
- *Students will able to identify present perfect continuous tense in sentence.*
- *Students will learn the form of verb used in present perfect continuous tense.*
- *Students will make keynotes regarding structure of present perfect continuous tense.*

KEY POINTS OF PRESENT PERFECT CONTINUOUS TENSE

Present perfect continuous tense is also known as present perfect progressive tense . It denotes something that started in past is still continuing in present .

It is mandatory to acknowledge that helping verb has/ have been following main verb first form + ing is key element in construction of sentences related to present perfect continuous tense.

Note* Helping verb has been is used with singular.

Helping verb have been is used with plural and I .

STRUCTURE OF PRESENT PERFECT CONTINUOUS TENSE

To access in deep the rules of present perfect continuous tense it is necessary to understand its structure.

RULE IN CASE OF AFFIRMATIVE SENTENCE

Subject + has / have + been + main verb first form + ing + object + since/ for + time.

Note* **" Since"** is used with definite and fixed times. Such as particular date , since morning etc.

"For" is used with indefinite time.

Illustration :

• I have been waiting for your call since morning .

Subject = I
Helping verb Has/ have been = have been
Main verb first form = wait
+
ing
object = for you
Since/for = since
Timing = morning

• She has been finding pink dress since morning

Subject= she
Helping verb Has/have been = has been
Main verb first form= find
+
ing

object = pink dress
since/for= since
Timing = morning

- He has been reading Romeo Juliet for two days.

  Subject= He
  Helping verb Has/have been = has been
  Main verb first form= read
  +
  ing
  object = Romeo Juliet
  since/for= for
  Timing = two days

- The Poet has been writing poem since morning.

  Subject= The poet
  Helping verb Has/have been = has been
  Main verb first form= write
  +
  ing
  object = poem
  since/for= since
  Timing = morning

- I have been watching movie since 9P.M

  Subject= I
  Helping verb Has/have been = have been
  Main verb first form= watch
  +
  ing

object = movie
since/for= since
Timing = 9 PM
SOME MORE EXAMPLES:

1. I have been watching concert for an hour.
2. He has been studying in the library for three hours.
3. He has been playing flute since morning.
4. We have been studying since 8o 'clock.
5. They have been living in Kolkata since 1970.
6. I have been writing assignments since morning.
7. We have been working for two years.
8. I have been preparing for competitive exams for three years.
9. I have been trying to learn the English language for three months.
10. She has been trying to paint walls since morning.

RULE IN CASE OF NEGATIVE SENTENCES
Subject + has/ have + not + been + main verb first form+ ing + object + since/ for + timing .

- I have not been studying English for three days.

subject = I
Has/have= have
not
been
main verb first form= study
+
ing
object = English
Since/ for= for

timing = three days

- They have not been living in Kolkata since 1970.

  subject = They
  Has/have= have
  not
  been
  main verb first form= live
  +
  ing
  object= in kolkata
  Since/ for= since
  timing= 1970

- He has not been reading Romeo Juliet for two days.

  subject = He
  Has/have = has
  not
  been
  main verb first form= read
  +
  ing
  object= Romeo Juliet
  Since/ for= for
  timing= two days

- The poet has not been writing environmental poem since morning.

  subject = The poet
  Has/have = has

not
been
main verb first form= write
+
ing
object= environmental poem
Since/ for= since
timing= morning

- I have not been writing assignments since morning.

subject = I
Has/have= have
not
been
main verb first form= write
+
ing
object = assignments
Since/ for= since
timing= morning

SOME MORE EXAMPLES

1. It has not been raining since morning.
2. He has not been watching movie since evening.
3. They have not been working for two years.
4. We have not been studying since 8o 'clock.
5. They have not been living in Uttrakhand since 2000.
6. I have not been watching concert for an hour.
7. He has not been studying in the library for three hours.
8. Raman has been waiting for her friend in park for the last two hours.
9. I have not been swimming in pool for years.

10. Dog has not been barking at stranger since tonight.

   RULE IN CASE OF INTERROGATIVE SENTENCES
   Has / have+ subject + been + main verb first form +
ing + object + since/ for+ timing
   Illustration :

* Have I been watching T.V. since evening ?

   Has / have= Have
   Subject = I
   been
   main verb first form = watch
   +
   ing
   object = T.V
   Since/for = Since
   timing = evening

* Has dog been barking at stranger since tonight?

   Has / have= Has
   Subject = dog
   been
   main verb first form = bark
   +
   ing
   object = stranger
   Since/for = since
   timing = tonight

* Have I been watching concert for an hour?

Has / have= Have
Subject = I
been
main verb first form = watch
+
ing
object = concert
Since/for = for
timing = an hour
SOME MORE EXAMPLE

1. Have I been working on this project since 10 January?
2. Have I been playing with a football since morning?
3. Has dog been swimming in pool for three hours?
4. Has It not been raining since morning?
5. Have they been sleeping since afternoon?
6. Have we been studying for competitive exams for three months?
7. Have you been running at Marathon since morning?
8. Has he been cooking continental dishes for years?
9. Have I been driving on road since evening?
10. Have I been reading newspaper since morning?

RULE IN CASE OF DOUBLE INTERROGATIVE SENTENCES

WH family + Has / have+ subject + been + main verb first form + ing + object + since/ for+ timing

Note – "WH family" includes-
Who
What
Where
When
Why

Which

How

Illustration:

- Why has dog been barking at stranger since tonight?

  WH family= Why
  Has / have = has
  subject= dog
  been
  main verb first form= bark
  +
  ing
  object= at stranger
  Since/for= since
  Timing= tonight

- Why have I been wasting my time for three days?

  WH family= Why
  Has / have = have
  subject= I
  been
  main verb first form= waste
  +
  ing
  object= my time
  Since/for= for
  Timing= three days
  SOME MORE EXAMPLES

1. What has he been studying since 4' o clock ?
2. What have you been doing here for 3 days?

3.   Why has this child been crying for 2 hours?
4.   Why have they been wasting their energy on rubbish project for few hours?
5.   When have they been sleeping since afternoon?
6.   Where has it been raining since morning?
7.   Why have the students been making noise for two hours?
8.   Where have they been waiting for me since 9 AM?
9.   Why has she not been taking rest for the last five days?
10. Where has she been teaching since September?

EVALUATION

1.   Construct ten sentences using present perfect continuous tense.

1.   ONE WORD QUERY

   a.   What helping verbs are used in present perfect continuous tense............
   b.   What form of verb is used in present perfect continuous tense.........
   c.   Since is used with........
   d.   For is used with..........

3.MAKE NOTES

a.   Affirmative sentence structure of present perfect continuous tense.
b.   Negative sentence structure of present perfect continuous tense.
c.   Interrogative sentence structure of present perfect continuous tense.

ANKITA SINGH

CHAPTER SIX

PAST INDEFINITE TENSE

OBJECTIVES OF STUDY

- *Students will learn concept of past indefinite tense.*
- *Students will acknowledge techniques to identify past Indefinite tense.*
- *Students will make keynotes regarding structure of past indefinite tense.*
- *Students will able to construct sentences using past indefinite tense.*

KEY POINTS OF PAST INDEFINITE TENSE

The past indefinite tense is also called simple past tense , it depict the action completed in past.

Second form of verb is always used in past indefinite tense.

The past indefinite tense is used to indicate past habits .

Example : She studied many hours every fortnight.

STRUCTURE OF PAST INDEFINITE TENSE

To understand past indefinite tense thoroughly let's have a look on structure of past indefinite or simple past tense.

RULE IN CASE OF AFFIRMATIVE SENTENCE
Subject + main verb second form + object
Illustrations:

- Arnav sang a song .

  Let's break the sentence to access its parts -
  Subject= Arnav
  Main verb second form = sang
  Object= a song

- I washed my shoes.

  Subject = I
  Main verb second form= Washed
  Object= my shoes

- She finished her assignment.

  Subject = She
  Main verb second form = finished
  object= her assignment

- I wrote a song.

  Subject = I
  Main verb second form = wrote
  object= a song
  SOME MORE EXAMPLES

1. It rained today.
2. They called me.
3. She cleared her test.

4.   I played yesterday.
5.   We met him.
6.   She ran very slow.
7.   He could not run.

RULE IN CASE OF NEGATIVE SENTENCE
Subject +did+ not + main verb first form + object
Illustrations :

• Radha did not eat grapes.

Subject= Radha
Did = did
not
Main verb First form = eat
Object = grapes

• Dogs did not eat sweets.

Subject= Dogs
Did
not
Main verb First form = eat
Object = sweets

• Sumit did not know English.

subject= Sumit
Did
not
Main verb First form = know
Object = English
SOME MORE EXAMPLES

1. I did not go to gym.
2. Ram did not know pali language.
3. Arvind did not grow crops.
4. Radha did not browse internet.
5. She did not play pub g .
6. They did not debate in public.
7. I did not know German.
8. Sita did not eat mango.
9. She did not know the art of cooking.
10. They did not like rabbit.

RULE IN CASE OF INTERROGATIVE SENTENCES
Did + subject +main verb first form + object ?
Illustration :

- Did she likes tea ?

  Did = Did
  Subject = she
  Main verb first form = likes
  object = tea

- Did you know German language ?

  Did = Did
  Subject = you
  Main verb first form = know
  object= German Language
  SOME MORE EXAMPLES

1. Did he develop android apps?
2. Did he use social media ?
3. Did you know English grammar?

4. Did Radha likes coffee?
5. Did farmer grow crops?
6. Did dog sleeps on cozy bed?
7. Did they sell mobile cover?
8. Did they play pub g?
9. Did Ram lives in Ayodhya?
10. Did you like burger?

RULE IN CASE OF DOUBLE INTERROGATIVE SENTENCES

WH family + did +subject +main verb first form + object

Note – "WH family" includes-
Who
What
Where
When
Why
Which
How
Illustration

• How did you know him ?

WH family = How
Did
Subject = you
Main verb first form =know
Object= him
SOME MORE EXAMPLE

1. Where did they live?
2. Why did he use social media?

3. Why did you like burger?
4. How did you know me?
5. Why did they play pub g?
6. Why did they sell mobile cover?
7. Why did Radha eat ice cream?
8. How did they ride bicycle?
9. What did your brother do ?
10. What did your mother bake in the microwave ?

EVALUATION

1. Make ten sentences using past indefinite tense.

1. Find out affirmative, negative, interrogative, double interrogative sentences from mix examples of past indefinite tense .

a. She came .
b. We met them.
c. We did not sleep in the courtyard.
d. They did not fight with their brothers.
e. Did Nishant go to school daily ?
f. Where did you live ?
g. Did your grandfather know English ?

CHAPTER SEVEN

PAST CONTINUOUS TENSE

OBJECTIVES OF STUDY

- *Students will learn the concept and rule of past continuous tense.*
- *Students will able to identify past continuous tense in sentences.*
- *Students will learn the form of verb used in past continuous tense.*
- *Students will make keynotes regarding structure of past continuous tense.*
- *Students will able to construct sentences using past continuous tense.*

KEY POINTS TO REMEMBER IN PAST CONTINUOUS TENSE

Past continuous tense refers to past progressive tense. It denotes continuing action that was happening at some point in the past.

It is mandatory to acknowledge that in main verb first form + ing is key element in construction of sentences related to past continuous tense.

STRUCTURE OF PAST CONTINUOUS TENSE

To understand past continuous tense in detail its essential to study its sentence structure.

RULE IN CASE OF AFFIRMATIVE SENTENCE

Subject + was/ were + main verb first form + ing + object

Note : * " was is used with singular , were is used with plural".

Illustration :

* Hemant was doing meditation .

  Subject = Hemant
  was/were = was
  Main verb first form= do
  +
  ing
  object = meditation

* Dog was eating calcium.

  Subject = Dog
  was/ were = was
  Main verb first form= eat
  +
  ing
  object = calcium

* Radha was writing letter.

  Subject = Radha
  was/ were = was
  Main verb first form= write

+

ing

object = letter

- we were playing cricket .

  Subject = we
  was/were = were
  Main verb first form= play
  +
  ing
  object = cricket

- Ram was watching movie.

  Subject = Ram
  was/ were = was
  Main verb first form= watch
  +
  ing
  object = movie

SOME MORE EXAMPLES

1. Shyam was playing flute.
2. Tammana was eating popcorn.
3. Doves were swimming in pool.
4. They were fighting for pencil.
5. Daisy was knitting cap.
6. Raghav was doing homework.
7. Gaurav was watching T.V.
8. Mr. Arnav was attending conference.
9. Anu was drinking coffee.
10. we were listening old commentaries.

Note : * In Past continuous tense we always use " Main verb first form + ing .

Example – Learn (Main verb 1st form) + ing _____ Learning.

Sing (Main verb 1st form) + ing _____ singing.

Dance (Main verb 1st form) + ing _____ Dancing.

Fight(Main verb 1st form) + ing _____ Fighting

RULE IN CASE OF NEGATIVE SENTENCES

Subject + was/were + not + main verb first form + ing + object

- She was not reading Newspaper.

  Subject= she
  was/ were = was
  not
  Main verb first form = read
  +
  ing
  Object= newspaper

- He was not doing painting.

  Subject= He
  was/ were= was
  not
  Main verb first form = do
  +
  ing
  Object= painting

- They were not playing cricket.

Subject= They
was/ were= were
not
Main verb first form = play
+
ing
Object= cricket

- Raman was not learning English

Subject= Raman
was/ were= was
not
Main verb first form = learn
+
ing
Object= English

SOME MORE EXAMPLES

1. Tammana was not eating popcorn.
2. Doves were not swimming in pool.
3. They were not fighting for pencil.
4. Daisy was not knitting cap.
5. Raghav was not doing homework.
6. Gaurav was not watching T.V.
7. Mr. Arnav was not attending conference.
8. Anurag was not drinking coffee.
9. He was not listening old commentaries.
10. They were not going to Mumbai.

RULE IN CASE OF INTERROGATIVE SENTENCE
was/ were + subject + main verb first form + ing +
object

- were they going to New Delhi ?

  was/ were = were
  Subject= they
  Main verb first form= go
  +
  ing
  Object= New Delhi

- was She Playing foot ball?

  was/ were = was
  Subject= she
  Main verb first form= play
  +
  ing
  Object= football

- Was he surfing internet?

  Was/ were = was
  Subject= he
  Main verb first form= surf
  +
  ing
  Object= internet

- Was she writing letter?

  Was/ were = was
  Subject= she
  Main verb first form= write
  +

ing
Object= letter

- Was dog sleeping outside?

Was / were = was
Subject= dog
Main verb first form= sleep
+
ing
Object= outside

SOME MORE EXAMPLES

1. Were they baking cake?
2. Was she going to school?
3. Was tiger playing with cubs?
4. Were boys playing chess?
5. Was he dancing on floor?
6. Was kamal taking tea?
7. Were they walking in the park?
8. Was Zoo administration bringing new zebra?
9. Was she painting daffodils ?
10. Were they making squash ?

RULE IN CASE OF DOUBLE INTERROGATIVE SENTENCE

WH family +was/ were + subject + main verb first form + ing + object

Note – "WH family" includes-

Who

What

Where

When

Why
Which
How

- Why were they going to New Delhi ?

  WH family= why
  Helping verb was/ were = were
  Subject= they
  Main verb first form = go
  +
  ing
  Object= to New Delhi

- Why was she watching T.V. ?

  WH family= Why
  Helping verb was/ were = was
  Subject= She
  Main verb first form= watch
  +
  ing
  object = T.V

SOME MORE EXAMPLES

1. Why were they baking cake?
2. When was she going to Mumbai ?
3. Where was tiger playing with cubs?
4. Why were boys playing chess?
5. Why were they dancing on floor?
6. What was she doing with T.V remote ?
7. How was he going to village ?
8. Where was she going today ?

9. Why was she eating toffee ?
10. Why was Radha fighting with Ramesh?
11. Why is Tarun sleeping on floor?

Evaluation

1. Construct ten sentences using past continuous tense.
2. Find out affirmative, negative, interrogative, double interrogative sentences from mix examples of past continuous tenses

- Ducks were not swimming in river.
- Manoj was not throwing garbage .
- Was Mohan writing letter?
- WasAshman playing video game?
- Was going to grandfather's house?
- Why was she painting landscape?
- Why was he eating medicine?

CHAPTER EIGHT

PAST PERFECT TENSE

OBJECTIVES OF STUDY

- *Students will understand the concept of past perfect tense.*
- *Students will learn the rules related to past perfect tense.*
- *Students will able to identify past perfect tense in sentence.*
- *Students will learn the form of verb used in past perfect tense.*
- *Students will make keynotes regarding structure of past perfect tense.*
- *Students will able to construct sentences using past perfect tense.*

KEY POINTS TO REMEMBER IN PAST PERFECT TENSE

Past perfect tense denotes action completed in past. It refers to action that was completed before the another action took place.

It is essential to acknowledge that main verb third form is key element in construction of sentences related to past perfect tense.

RULE IN CASE OF AFFIRMATIVE SENTENCE

To understand past perfect tense in detail its essential to study structure of past perfect tense .

Subject + had + main verb third form +object.
Illustration :

- I had taken medicine .

  Subject= I
  had
  Main verb third form = taken
  Object = medicine

- He had eaten my cake.

  Subject= He
  had
  Main verb third form = eaten
  Object = my cake

- They had bought a red car.

  Subject= They
  had
  Main verb third form = bought
  Object = red car

- We had met him.

  Subject= we
  had
  Main verb third form = met
  Object = him

- Raman had beaten my puppy .

Subject= Raman
had
Main verb third form = beaten
Object = my puppy
SOME MORE EXAMPLE

1. She had forgotten her bag.
2. He had taken my pencil.
3. He had finished his manuscript.
4. She had lost her wedding ring.
5. He had broken his left hand.
6. Rohan had started new job.
7. Diksha had forgotten English tenses.
8. We had met him.
9. I had seen blue birds.
10. He had reached London.

RULE IN CASE OF NEGATIVE SENTENCE
Subject + had + not+ main verb third form + object
Illustration

- I had not seen blue birds.

Subject= I
had
not
Main verb third form = seen
Object = blue birds

- He had not reached office.

Subject = He
had

not
Main verb third form = reached
Object = office

- Diksha had not eaten Mango.

  Subject = Diksha
  had
  not
  Main verb third form = eaten
  Object = Mango

- He had not taken my pencil.

  Subject = He
  had
  not
  Main verb third form = taken
  Object = my pencil

- We had not met him.

  Subject = we
  had
  not
  Main verb third form = met
  Object = him

SOME MORE EXAMPLES

1. She had not forgotten her bag.
2. He had not taken my book.
3. He had not finished his manuscript.
4. She had not lost her wedding ring.

5. He had not broken his leg.
6. Rohan had not started a new job.
7. Ram had not forgotten my name.
8. We had not met him.
9. I had not seen blue birds.
10. He had not reached home.

RULE IN CASE OF INTERROGATIVE SENTENCE
Had + subject + main verb third form + object

- Had you won the football match ?

  Had
  Subject= you
  Main verb third form= won
  Object = foot ball match ?

- Had you written assignments ?

  Had
  Subject= you
  Main verb third form= written
  Object= Assignment ?

- Had you seen blue birds?

  Had
  subject = you
  Main verb third form = seen
  object = blue birds

- Had she written manuscript?

Had
Subject= she
Main verb third form= written
Object= manuscript?

- Had he beaten my puppy ?

Had
subject = he
Main verb third form = beaten
object= my puppy

SOME MORE EXAMPLES

1. Had they ever played pub g?
2. Had Anant missed the bus ?
3. Had she visited U.K?
4. Had he sent you letter?
5. Had you ever seen Tiger ?
6. Had they taken camel ride?
7. Had you done your homework ?
8. Had they met Professor Shaw?
9. Had she taken medicine?
10. Had Ram learnt Psychology ?

RULE IN CASE OF DOUBLE INTERROGATIVE SENTENCE

WH Family + had+ subject + main verb third form + object

Note * WH Family includes:

Who
What
Where
When

Why
Which
How
Who
What
Where
When
Why
Which
How
Illustration:

- When had you won the trophy?

  WH family = when
  had
  Subject = you
  Main verb third form = won
  Object = the trophy

- How had you done the homework?

  WH family = How
  had
  Subject = you
  Main verb third form = done
  Object = the homework

- Where had you met Mr. Brown Nicolas ?

  WH family = where
  had
  Subject= you

Main verb third form = met
Object = Mr. Brown Nicolas

- Where had you seen blue birds?

WH family = where
had
Subject= you
Main verb third form = seen
Object = blue birds
SOME MORE EXAMPLES

1. Why had she not came home?
2. Why had she not taken bed rest?
3. where had you seen white tiger?
4. How had you done your assignment ?
5. Why had she beaten your pet ?
6. Why had she taken your notebook ?
7. Where had they went yesterday ?
8. How had they managed the tight budget ?i
9. when had they developed android app ?
10. where had you watched the drama?

EVALUATION

1. Write ten sentence related to past perfect tense

1. One word query

a. which form of verb is used in past perfect tense............
b. write affirmative sentence structure in context of past perfect tense.......

c. Write negative sentence structure in context of past perfect tense......

CHAPTER NINE

PAST PERFECT CONTINUOUS TENSE

OBJECTIVES OF STUDY

- *Students will understand the concept of past perfect continuous tense.*
- *Students will acknowledge rules to construct sentences related to past perfect continuous tense.*
- *Students will able to identify past perfect continuous tense in sentence.*
- *Students will learn the form of verb used in past perfect continuous tense.*
- *Students will make keynotes regarding structure of past perfect continuous tense*

KEY POINTS OF PAST PERFECT CONTINUOUS TENSE

Past perfect continuous tense is also known as past perfect progressive tense. It denotes action that started in past and continued in the past for some time.

It is mandatory to acknowledge that helping verb had been following main verb first form + ing is key element in construction of sentences related to past perfect continuous tense.

Note* Helping verb had been is used in past perfect continuous tense.

STRUCTURE OF PAST PERFECT CONTINUOUS TENSE

To access in deep the rules of past perfect continuous tense it is necessary to understand its structure.

RULE IN CASE OF AFFIRMATIVE SENTENCE

Subject + had been + main verb first form + ing + object + since/ for + time.

Note* " Since" is used with definite and fixed times. Such as particular date , since morning etc.

"For" is used with indefinite time.

Illustration :

- I had been waiting for you since morning .

Subject = I
Helping verb Had been = had been
Main verb first form = wait
+
ing
object = for you
Since/for = since
Timing = morning

- She had been finding pink dress since morning.

Subject= she
Helping verb Had been = had been
Main verb first form= find
+
ing

object = pink dress
since/for= since
Timing = morning

- He had been reading Romeo Juliet for two days.

    Subject= He
    Helping verb Had been = had been
    Main verb first form= read
    +
    ing
    object = Romeo Juliet
    since/for= for
    Timing = two days

- The Poet had been writing poem since morning.

    Subject= The poet
    Helping verb Had been = had been
    Main verb first form= write
    +
    ing
    object = poem
    since/for= since
    Timing = morning

- I had been watching movie since 9P.M

    Subject= I
    Helping verb Had been = had been
    Main verb first form= watch
    +
    ing

object = movie
since/for= since
Timing = 9 PM
SOME MORE EXAMPLES:

1. I had been watching concert for an hour.
2. He had been studying in the library for three hours.
3. He had been playing flute since morning.
4. We had been studying since 8o 'clock.
5. They had been living in Kolkata since 1970.
6. I had been writing assignments since morning.
7. We had been working for two years.
8. I had been preparing for competitive exams for three years.
9. I had been trying to learn the English language for three months.
10. She had been trying to paint walls since morning.

RULE IN CASE OF NEGATIVE SENTENCES
Subject + had + not + been + main verb first form+ ing + object + since/ for + timing .

- I had not been studying English for three days.

subject = I
had
not
been
main verb first form= study
+
ing
object = English
Since/ for= for

timing = three days

- They had not been living in Kolkata since 1970.

subject = They
had
not
been
main verb first form= live
+
ing
object= in kolkata
Since/ for= since
timing= 1970

- He had not been reading Romeo Juliet for two days.

subject = He
had
not
been
main verb first form= read
+
ing
object= Romeo Juliet
Since/ for= for
timing= two days

- The poet had not been writing environmental poem since morning.

subject = The poet
had

not

been

main verb first form= write

+

ing

object= environmental poem

Since/ for= since

timing= morning

- I had not been writing assignments since morning.

subject = I

had

not

been

main verb first form= write

+

ing

object = assignments

Since/ for= since

timing= morning

SOME MORE EXAMPLES

1. It had not been raining since morning.
2. He had not been watching movie since evening.
3. They had not been working for two years.
4. We had not been studying since 8o 'clock.
5. They had not been living in Uttrakhand since 2000.
6. I had not been watching concert for an hour.
7. He had not been studying in the library for three hours.
8. Raman had been waiting for her friend in park for the last two hours.
9. I had not been swimming in pool for years.

10. Dog had not been barking at stranger since tonight.

RULE IN CASE OF INTERROGATIVE SENTENCES
Had + subject + been + main verb first form + ing + object + since/ for+ timing
Illustration :

• Had I been watching T.V. since evening ?

Had
Subject = I
been
main verb first form = watch
+
ing
object = T.V
Since/for = Since
timing = evening

• Had dog been barking at stranger since tonight?

Had
Subject = dog
been
main verb first form = bark
+
ing
object = stranger
Since/for = since
timing = tonight

• Had I been watching concert for an hour?

Had
Subject = I
been
main verb first form = watch
+
ing
object = concert
Since/for = for
timing = an hour
SOME MORE EXAMPLE

1. Had I been working on this project since 10 January?
2. Had I been playing with a football since morning?
3. Had dog been swimming in pool for three hours?
4. Had It not been raining since morning?
5. Had they been sleeping since afternoon?
6. Had we been studying for competitive exams for three months?
7. Had you been running at Marathon since morning?
8. Had he been cooking continental dishes for years?
9. Had I been driving on road since evening?
10. Had I been reading newspaper since morning?

RULE IN CASE OF DOUBLE INTERROGATIVE SENTENCES

WH family + Had + subject + been + main verb first form + ing + object + since/ for+ timing

Note – "WH family" includes-

Who

What

Where

When

Why

Which

How

Illustration:

- Why had dog been barking at stranger since tonight?

  WH family= Why
  had
  subject= dog
  been
  main verb first form= bark
  +
  ing
  object= at stranger
  Since/for= since
  Timing= tonight

- Why had I been wasting my time for three days?

  WH family= Why
  had
  subject= I
  been
  main verb first form= waste
  +
  ing
  object= my time
  Since/for= for
  Timing= three days

SOME MORE EXAMPLES

1. What had he been studying since 4' o clock ?
2. What had you been doing here for 3 days?

3. Why had this child been crying for 2 hours?
4. Why had they been wasting their energy on rubbish project for few hours?
5. When had they been sleeping since afternoon?
6. Where had it been raining since morning?
7. Why had the students been making noise for two hours?
8. Where had they been waiting for me since 9 AM?
9. Why had she not been taking rest for the last five days?
10. Where had she been teaching since September?

EVALUATION

1. Construct ten sentences using past perfect continuous tense.

1. ONE WORD QUERY

   a. What helping verbs are used in past perfect continuous tense............
   b. What form of verb is used in past perfect continuous tense.........
   c. Since is used with........
   d. For is used with..........

3.MAKE NOTES

a. Affirmative sentence structure of past perfect continuous tense.
b. Negative sentence structure of past perfect continuous tense.
c. Interrogative sentence structure of past perfect continuous tense.

CHAPTER TEN

FUTURE INDEFINITE TENSE

OBJECTIVES OF STUDY

- *Students will learn concept of future indefinite tense.*
- *Students will acknowledge techniques to identify future Indefinite tense.*
- *Students will make keynotes regarding structure of future indefinite tense.*
- *Students will able to construct sentences using future indefinite tense.*

KEY POINTS OF FUTURE INDEFINITE TENSE

Simple future tense or future indefinite tense indicates that an action has not occurred yet but will take place at some point in future.

CONCEPT OF MODAL VERB IMPORTANT IN FUTURE INDEFINITE TENSE

- Shall is used with I and We.
- Will is used with rest all except I and we.
- Exception - In case of sentences expressing promises , determination, Threat etc the rule reverse, i.e Instead of

shall will with be used with I and we .

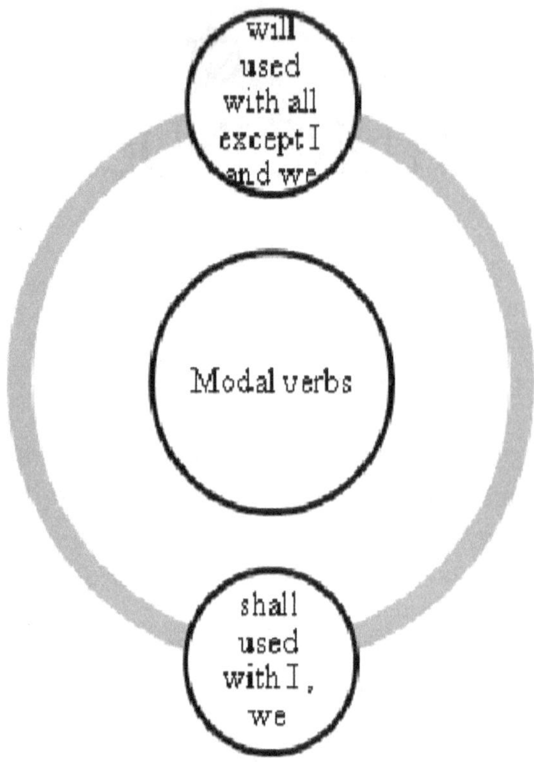

Concept of Modal verbs
RULE IN CASE OF AFFIRMATIVE SENTENCE
Subject + will/ shall + main verb first form + object
Illustrations:

• Aryan will play football.

Let's break the sentence to access its parts
Subject = Aryan
Modal verb
Will/ shall = will
Main verb first form= play
Object = football

- I shall write a poem.

  Subject = I
  Modal verb
  Will/ shall = shall
  Main verb first form = write
  Object = a poem

- Rohan will eat a candy.

  Subject = Rohan
  Modal verb
  Will/ shall = will
  Main verb first form = eat
  Object = a candy

- Teacher will read poem.

  Subject = Teacher
  Modal verb
  Will/ shall = will
  Main verb first form = read
  Object = poem
  SOME MORE EXAMPLES

1. I shall write article on current topics.

2. I shall love to listen old songs.
3. He will love to travel around the globe.
4. He will sing a song .
5. Arun will make coffee.
6. She will prefer milk to cornflakes.
7. She will read everyday.
8. Here will come the aircraft!
9. He will bring rose every morning.
10. The train will leave at 6:30 PM.

RULE IN CASE OF NEGATIVE SENTENCE
Subject + will / shall+ not + main verb first form + object
Illustrations :

- Radha will not like grapes.

Subject= Radha
Modal verb
Will/ shall = will
Not
Main verb First form = like
Object = grapes

- Ducks will not swim today.

Subject = Ducks
Modal verb
Will/ shall = will
Not
Main verb First form = swim
Object = today

- Sumit will not eat Mango.

  Subject = Sumit
  Modal verb
  Will/ shall = will
  Not
  Main verb first form = eat
  Object = mango
  SOME MORE EXAMPLES

1. I shall not go to gym.
2. Ram will not know the secret .
3. Arvind will not grow crops.
4. Radha will not browse internet.
5. She will not play pub g .
6. They will not debate in public.
7. I shall not know German.
8. Sita will not eat mango.
9. She will not know the art of cooking.
10. He will not like rabbit.

RULE IN CASE OF INTERROGATIVE SENTENCES
Will/ shall + subject +main verb first form + object ?
Illustration :

- will she make tea ?

  Modal verb
  Will/ shall = will
  Subject = she
  Main verb first form = make
  object =tea ?
  SOME MORE EXAMPLES

1. will he develop android apps?
2. Shall I use social media ?
3. Shall I know English grammar?
4. Will Radha like coffee art ?
5. Will farmer grow crops?
6. Will dog sleep on cozy bed?
7. Will Anirudh sell mobile cover?
8. Shall I play pub g?
9. Will Ram lives in Ayodhya?
10. Will he like burger?

RULE IN CASE OF DOUBLE INTERROGATIVE SENTENCES

WH family + will / shall +subject +main verb first form + object

Note – "WH family" includes-
Who
What
Where
When
Why
Which
How
Illustration

• How will she manage naughty kids ?

WH family = How
Modal verb
Will / shall = will
Subject = she
Main verb first form = manage
Object = naughty kids.

SOME MORE EXAMPLE

1. Where will he stay tonight?
2. How will he use social media?
3. Why shall I like burger?
4. How will he know me?
5. Why shall I play pub g?
6. Why will she sell mobile cover?
7. Why shall I eat ice cream?
8. Why shall I ride bicycle?
9. What will your brother do ?
10. What will Ram bake in the microwave ?

EVALUATION

1. Make ten sentences using future indefinite tense.

1. Find out affirmative, negative, interrogative, double interrogative sentences from mix examples of present indefinite tense .

- What will your brother do ?
- She will not know the art of cooking.
- He will not eat breakfast.
- Raman will eat chocobar.
- Rohan will dance on floor.

CHAPTER ELEVEN

FUTURE CONTINUOUS TENSE

OBJECTIVES OF STUDY

- *Students will learn the concept and rule of future continuous tense.*
- *Students will able to identify future continuous tense in sentences.*
- *Students will learn the form of verb used in future continuous tense.*
- *Students will make keynotes regarding structure of future continuous tense.*
- *Students will able to construct sentences using future continuous tense.*

KEY POINTS TO REMEMBER IN FUTURE CONTINUOUS TENSE

Future continuous tense is also called future progressive tense. It denotes action that happens in future and may continue for an expected period of time.

It is mandatory to acknowledge that modal verb shall / will followed by auxiliary verb be and main verb first form + ing is key element in construction of sentences related to future continuous tense.

CONCEPT OF MODAL VERB IMPORTANT IN FUTURE CONTINUOUS TENSE

- Shall is used with I and We.
- Will is used with rest all except I and we.
- Exception - In case of sentences expressing promises , determination, Threat etc the rule reverse, i.e Instead of shall will with be used with I and we .

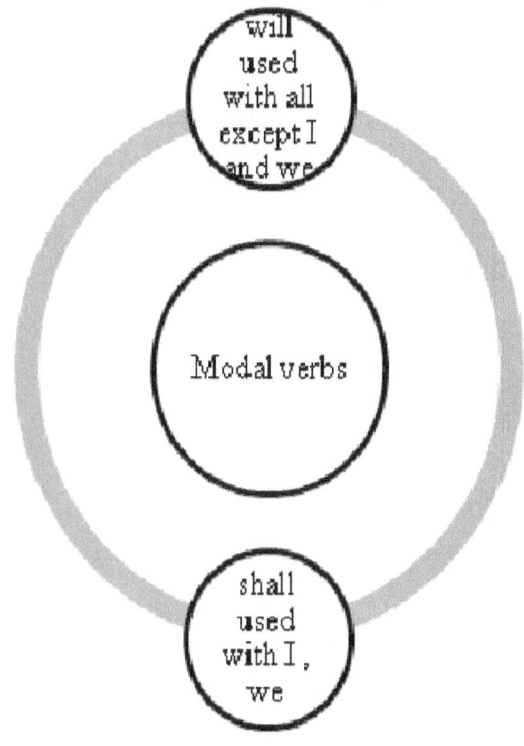

STRUCTURE OF FUTURE CONTINUOUS TENSE

To understand future continuous tense in detail its essential to study structure of future continuous tense .

RULE IN CASE OF AFFIRMATIVE SENTENCE

Subject + shall / will +be + main verb first form + ing + object

Illustration :

- Kajal will be doing yoga.

    Subject= Kajal
    Modal verb Will/ shall = will
    Be
    Main verb first form = do
    +
    Ing
    Object = yoga

- I shall be writing letter.

    Subject = I
    Modal verb Will/ shall = shall
    Be
    Main verb first form = Write
    +
    Ing
    Object = letter

- He will be coming home

    Subject = He
    Modal verb
    Will/ shall = will

Be
Main verb first form= come
+
Ing
Object = home
SOME MORE EXAMPLES

1. Shyam will be playing flute.
2. Tammana will be eating popcorn.
3. Doves will be swimming in pool.
4. Raman will be fighting for pencil.
5. I shall be knitting cap.
6. Raghav will be doing homework.
7. Gaurav will be watching T.V.
8. Mr. Arnav will be attending conference.
9. Anu will be drinking coffee.
10. I shall be listening old commentaries.

RULE IN CASE OF NEGATIVE SENTENCES
Subject + shall / will + not +be + main verb first form
+ ing + object
Illustration :

- She will not be reading Newspaper.

Subject = she
Modal verb Will/ shall= will
Not
Be
Main verb
first form= read
+
Ing

Object = newspaper
SOME MORE EXAMPLES

1. Tammana will not be eating popcorn.
2. Doves will not be swimming in pool.
3. I shall not be fighting for pencil.
4. Daisy will not be knitting cap.
5. Raghav will not be doing homework.
6. Gaurav will not be watching T.V.
7. Mr. Arnav will not be attending conference.
8. Anurag will not be drinking coffee.
9. I shall not be listening old commentaries.
10. I shall not be going to Mumbai.

RULE IN CASE OF INTERROGATIVE SENTENCE
Shall / will + subject +be + main verb first form + ing + object

- Shall I be going to New Delhi ?

Modal verb Will/ shall = shall
Subject= I
Be
Main verb first form =go
+
Ing
object= Delhi

- Shall I be surfing internet ?

Modal verb Will/ shall= shall
Subject= I
Be

Main verb first form= surf

+

Ing

Object= internet

SOME MORE EXAMPLES

1. Shall I be baking cake?
2. Will she be going to school?
3. Will tiger be playing with cubs?
4. Will boys be playing chess?
5. Shall I be dancing on floor?
6. Will kamal be taking tea?
7. Shall I be walking in the park?
8. Will Zoo administration be bringing new zebra?
9. Will she be painting daffodils ?
10. Will Tom be making squash ?

RULE IN CASE OF DOUBLE INTERROGATIVE SENTENCE

WH family + shall / will + subject + be + main verb first form + ing + object

Note – "WH family" includes-

Who

What

Where

When

Why

Which

How

- Where shall I be going today ?

WH family = Where

Modal verb Will / shall
Subject= I
Be
Main verb first form = go
+

ing
Object= today ?
SOME MORE EXAMPLES

1. Why shall I be baking cake?
2. When will she be going to Mumbai ?
3. Where will he be playing golf ?
4. Why will boys be wasting time ?
5. Why shall I be dancing on floor?
6. What shall I be doing to gain money ?
7. How will he be going to village ?
8. Where shall I be going today ?
9. Why will she be eating toffee .
10. Why will Radha be fighting with Ramesh ?

EVALUATION

1. Construct ten sentences using future continuous tense.

1. Find out affirmative, negative, interrogative, double interrogative sentences from mix examples of future continuous tense .

a. Why shall I be dancing on floor?
b. He will not be telling story.
c. My brother will not be riding bicycle .
d. Mr. Andrew will not be watching T.V.
e. Will tiger be playing with cubs.

f.   I shall not be listening old lyrics.

CHAPTER TWELVE

FUTURE PERFECT TENSE

OBJECTIVES OF STUDY

- *Students will understand the concept of future perfect tense.*
- *Students will learn the rules related to future perfect tense.*
- *Students will able to identify future perfect tense in sentence.*
- *Students will learn the form of verb used in future perfect tense.*
- *Students will make keynotes regarding structure of future perfect tense.*
- *Students will able to construct sentences using future perfect tense.*

KEY POINTS TO REMEMBER IN FUTURE PERFECT TENSE

Future perfect tense refers to a completed action in future. It is essential to acknowledge that modal verb will/ shall have followed by main verb third form is key element in construction of sentences related to future perfect tense.

CONCEPT OF MODAL VERB IMPORTANT IN FUTURE PERFECT TENSE

- Shall is used with I and We.
- Will is used with rest all except I and we.
- Exception - In case of sentences expressing promises , determination, Threat etc the rule reverse, i.e Instead of shall will with be used with I and we.

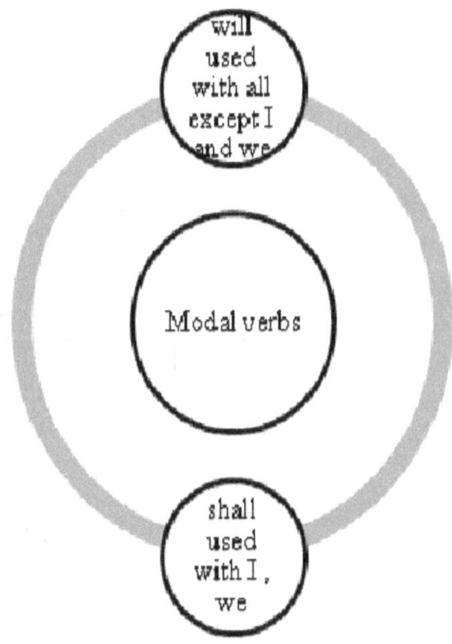

Concept of Modal verb

RULE IN CASE OF AFFIRMATIVE SENTENCE

To understand future perfect tense in detail its essential to study structure of future perfect tense .

Subject + will / shall + have + main verb third form +object.

Note*

Illustration :

- I shall have taken medicine .

subject = I
Modal verb Will/ shall= shall
Have
Main verb third form = taken
Object = medicine

- Amber will have bought a red car.

Subject= Amber
Modal verb Will/ shall= will
Have
Main verb third form = bought
Object = Red car

- We shall have met him.

Subject= We
Modal verb will/shall= shall
Have
Main verb third form= met
Object= him
SOME MORE EXAMPLE

1. She will have forgotten her bag.
2. He will have taken my pencil.

3. He will have finished his manuscript.
4. She will have lost her wedding ring.
5. He will have broken his left hand.
6. Rohan will have started new job.
7. Diksha will have forgotten English tenses.
8. We shall have met him.
9. I shall have seen blue birds.

He will have reached London

RULE IN CASE OF NEGATIVE SENTENCE

Subject + will / shall + not + have + main verb third form + object

Illustration

- I shall not have seen blue birds.

    Subject= I
    Modal verb will/ shall= shall
    Not
    Have
    Main verb third form= seen
    Object= blue birds

- He will not have reached office.

    Subject = He
    Modal verb will/ shall= will
    Not
    Have
    Main verb third form = reached
    object =office

- Diksha will not have eaten popcorn.

Subject = Diksha
Modal verb will/ shall= will
Not
Have
Main verb third form = eaten
object = popcorn

- He will not have taken pencil.

Subject = He
Modal verb will/ shall = will
Not
Have
Main verb third form = taken
object = pencil

- We shall not have met him.

Subject= we
Modal verb will/ shall = shall
Not
Have
Main verb third form= met
Object= him

SOME MORE EXAMPLES

1. She will not have forgotten her bag.
2. He will not have taken my book.
3. He will not have finished his manuscript.
4. She will not have lost her wedding ring.
5. He will not have broken his leg.
6. Rohan will not have started a new job.
7. Ram will not have forgotten my name.

8. We shall not have met him.
9. I shall not have seen blue birds.
10. I shall not have reached home.

RULE IN CASE OF INTERROGATIVE SENTENCE
Will / shall + subject + have +main verb third form + object

- Will Raman have won the football match ?

  Modal verb Will/ shall = Will
  Subject= Raman
  Have
  Main verb third form= won
  Object = the football match

- Shall I have written assignment ?

  Modal verb Will/ shall = Shall
  Subject= I
  Have
  Main verb third form = written
  Object= Assignment ?

- *Will he have stolen my money?*

  Modal verb Will/shall= Will
  Subject =He
  Have
  Main verb third form = Stolen
  Object= My money?
  SOME MORE EXAMPLES

1. Shall I have played pub g?
2. Will Anant have missed the bus ?
3. Will she have visited U.K?
4. Will he have sent you letter?
5. Will you have ever seen Tiger ?
6. Shall I have taken camel ride?
7. Will shruti have done your pending work ?
8. Shall I have met Professor Shaw?
9. Will she have taken medicine?
10. Will Ram have learnt Psychology ?

RULE IN CASE OF DOUBLE INTERROGATIVE SENTENCE

WH Family + will / shall + subject + have + main verb third form + object

Note * WH Family includes:

Who

What

Where

When

Why

Which

How

Who

What

Where

When

Why

Which

How

Illustration:

• When shall I have won the trophy?

WH family= When
Modal verb Will / shall = shall
Subject= I
Have
Main verb third form= won
Object= the trophy ?

- Where shall I *have* met Mr. Brown Nicolas ?

WH family = Where
Modal verb Will/shall= shall
Subject =I
Have
Main verb third form= met
Object = Mr. Brown Nicolas ?
SOME MORE EXAMPLES

1. Why shall I have came home?
2. Why will she have taken my workbook ?
3. where shall I have seen white tiger?
4. How will he have dispatched your consignment ?
5. Why will she have beaten your brother ?
6. Why will he have taken your notebook ?
7. How shall I have managed the tight budget ?
8. when will I have written manuscript ?
9. When will she have cooked food ?
10. where shall I have watched the drama?

EVALUATION
1.Write ten sentence related to future perfect tense
2.One word query

a. which form of verb is used in future perfect tense............

b. write affirmative sentence structure in context of future perfect tense.......

c. Write negative sentence structure in context of future perfect tense......

CHAPTER THIRTEEN

FUTURE PERFECT CONTINUOUS TENSE

OBJECTIVES OF STUDY

- *Students will understand the concept of future perfect continuous tense.*
- *Students will acknowledge rules to construct sentences related to future perfect continuous tense.*
- *Students will able to identify future perfect continuous tense in sentence.*
- *Students will learn the form of verb used in future perfect continuous tense.*
- *Students will make keynotes regarding structure of future perfect continuous tense.*

KEY POINTS OF PRESENT PERFECT CONTINUOUS TENSE

Future perfect continuous tense is also known as future perfect progressive tense . It denotes continuity of action, Any action that will continue up until a point in future.

It is mandatory to acknowledge that modal verb will/ shall with auxiliary verb have followed by been (third form of be) and main verb first form + ing is key element in construction of sentences related to future perfect continuous tense.

Example- I will have been working since 4 AM.

Let's break the sentence .

- I denotes subject.
- Will is modal verb in sentence.
- Have is auxiliary verb in sentence.
- Been is third form of be .
- Working denotes main verb first form + ing
- Since denotes definite time 4 AM

CONCEPT OF MODAL VERB USED IN FUTURE PERFECT CONTINUOUS TENSE

- Shall is used with I and We.
- Will is used with rest all except I and we.
- Exception - In case of sentences expressing promises , determination, Threat etc the rule reverse, i.e Instead of shall will with be used with I and we .

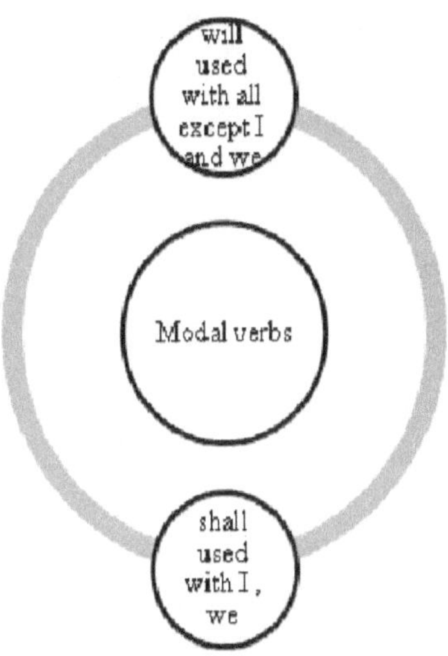

Concept of modal verb

STRUCTURE OF FUTURE PERFECT CONTINUOUS TENSE

To access in deep the rules of future perfect continuous tense it is necessary to understand its structure.

RULE IN CASE OF AFFIRMATIVE SENTENCE

Subject + will / shall +have been + main verb first form + ing + object + since/ for + time.

Note* " Since" is used with definite and fixed times. Such as particular date , since morning etc.

"For" is used with indefinite time.

Illustration :

- We shall have been reading book since morning.

Subject = We
Modal verb Will/ shall = shall
Helping verb have been = have been
Main verb first form = read
+
ing
object = book
Since/for = since
Timing = morning

- She will have been finding pink dress since morning .

Subject = She
Modal verb Will/ shall = will
Helping verb have been = have been
Main verb first form = find
+
ing
object = pink dress
Since/for = since
Timing = morning

- He will have been reading Romeo Juliet for two days.

Subject = He
Modal verb Will/ shall = will
Helping verb have been = have been
Main verb first form = read
+
ing
object = Romeo Juliet
Since/for = for
Timing = two days

- The poet will have been Writing poem since morning .

  Subject = The poet
  Modal verb Will/ shall = will
  Helping verb have been = have been
  Main verb first form = write
  +
  ing
  object = poem
  Since/for = since
  Timing = morning

- I shall have been watching movie since 9 P.M

  Subject = I
  Modal verb Will/ shall = Shall
  Helping verb have been = have been
  Main verb first form = watch
  +
  ing
  object = movie
  Since/for = since
  Timing = 9 P.M.
  SOME MORE EXAMPLES:

1. I shall have been watching concert for an hour.
2. He will have been studying in the library for three hours.
3. He will have been playing flute since morning.
4. We shall have been studying since 8o 'clock.
5. She will have been swimming in river for two hours.
6. I shall have been writing assignments since morning.
7. We shall have been working for two years.

8. I shall have been preparing for competitive exams for three years.
9. She will have been trying to learn the English language for three months.
10. She will have been trying to paint walls since morning.

RULE IN CASE OF NEGATIVE SENTENCES
Subject + will / shall+ not + have been + main verb first form+ ing + object + since/ for + timing .
Illustration :

- I shall not have been studying English for three days.

   subject= I
   Modal verb Will/ shall=Shall
   Not
   Helping verb have been= have been
   main verb first form= study
   +
   ing
   object= English
   Since/ for = for
   timing= three days.

- She will not have been living in Kolkata since 1970.

   subject= She
   Modal verb Will/ shall= will
   Not
   Helping verb have been= have been
   main verb first form= live
   +
   ing

object= Kolkata
Since/ for = since
timing= 1970

- He will not have been reading Romeo Juliet for two days.

  subject= He
  Modal verb Will/ shall= will
  Not
  Helping verb have been= have been
  main verb first form= read
  +
  ing
  object= Romeo Juliet
  Since/ for = for
  timing= two days

- The poet will not have been writing environmental poem since morning.

  subject= The poet
  Modal verb Will/ shall= will
  Not
  Helping verb have been= have been
  main verb first form= write
  +
  ing
  object= environmental poem
  Since/ for = since
  timing= morning

- I shall not have been writing assignments since morning.

subject= I
Modal verb Will/ shall= shall
Not
Helping verb have been= have been
main verb first form= write
+
ing
object= assignments
Since/ for = since
timing= morning
SOME MORE EXAMPLES

1. It will not have been raining since morning.
2. He will not have been watching movie since evening.
3. We shall not have been working for two years.
4. We shall not have been studying since 8o 'clock.
5. I shall not have been living in Uttrakhand since 2000.
6. I shall not have been watching concert for an hour.
7. He will not have been studying in the library for three hours.
8. Raman will not have been waiting for her friend in park for the last two hours.
9. I shall not have been swimming in pool for years.
10. Dog will not have been barking at stranger since tonight.

RULE IN CASE OF INTERROGATIVE SENTENCES
Will / shall + subject + have been + main verb first form + ing + object + since/ for+ timing
Illustration :

- Will she have been watching T.V. since evening ?

  Modal verb Will / shall = Will
  Subject= She
  Helping verb have been = have been
  main verb first form= watch
  ing
  object= T.V
  Since/for= Since
  timing= evening ?

- Will dog have been eating treat since tonight?

  Modal verb Will / shall = Will
  Subject= dog
  Helping verb have been= have been
  main verb first form= eat
  ing
  object= treat
  Since/for= since
  timing= tonight ?

- Shall I have been living in Uttrakhand since 2000?

  Modal verb Will / shall = Shall
  Subject= I
  Helping verb have been= have been
  main verb first form= live
  ing
  object= Uttrakhand
  Since/for= since
  timing= 2000 ?
  SOME MORE EXAMPLE

1. Shall I have been working on this project since 10 January?
2. Shall I have been playing with a football since morning?
3. Will dog have been swimming in pool for three hours?
4. Will It have been raining since morning?
5. Shall I have been sleeping since afternoon?
6. Shall we have been studying for competitive exams for three months?
7. Will she have been running at Marathon since morning?
8. Will he have been cooking continental dishes for years?
9. Will she have been driving on road since evening?

RULE IN CASE OF DOUBLE INTERROGATIVE SENTENCES

WH family + will / shall + subject + have been + main verb first form + ing + object + since/ for+ time

Note – "WH family" includes-

Who

What

Where

When

Why

Which

How

Illustration:

• Why will dog have been barking at stranger since tonight?

WH family =Why

Modal verb will/ shall= will

subject= dog

Helping verb have been= have been

main verb first form= bark
+
ing
object= stranger
Since/for = since
Timing= tonight

- Why will she have been writing my assignments for three days?

WH family =Why
Modal verb will/ shall= will
subject= she
Helping verb have been= have been
main verb first form= write
+
ing
object= my assignments
Since/for = for
Timing= three days ?

- Where will he have been performing drama since afternoon?

WH family =Where
Modal verb will/ shall= will
subject= he
Helping verb have been= have been
main verb first form= perform
+
ing
object= drama
Since/for = since

Timing= afternoon ?
SOME MORE EXAMPLES

1. What will he have been studying since 4' o clock ?
2. What will she have been doing here for 3 days?
3. Why will Renu have been crying for 2 hours?
4. Why shall I have been wasting their energy on rubbish project for few hours?
5. When will he have been sleeping since afternoon?
6. Where will it have been raining since morning?
7. Why will the students have been making noise for two hours?
8. Where will she have been waiting for me since 9 AM?
9. Why shall I have been driving car for the last few hours?
10. Where shall she have been teaching since September?

EVALUATION

1. Construct ten sentences using future perfect continuous tense.

1. ONE WORD QUERY

   a. What helping verbs are used in future perfect continuous tense............
   b. What form of verb is used in future perfect continuous tense.........
   c. What modal verbs are used in future perfect continuous tense ......
   d. Will is used with........
   e. Shall is used with......
   f. Since is used with........
   g. For is used with..........

3.MAKE NOTES

a. Affirmative sentence structure of future perfect continuous tense.
b. Negative sentence structure of future perfect continuous tense.
c. Interrogative sentence structure of future perfect continuous tense.

CHAPTER FOURTEEN

REVISION OF TENSES STRUCTURE

PRESENT INDEFINITE TENSE

AFFIRMATIVE SENTENCE

Subject+ main verb first form +es/s + object

NEGATIVE SENTENCE

Subject+do/does+ not+ main verb first form+ object

INTERROGATIVE SENTENCE

Do/ Does+ subject + main verb first form+ object ?

DOUBLE INTERROGATIVE SENTENCES

WH family+ Do/Does+ subject + main verb first form + object

PRESENT CONTINUOUS TENSE

AFFIRMATIVE SENTENCE

Subject+is/am/are+ main verb first form+ing+ object

NEGATIVE SENTENCES

Subject +is/am/are+ not+ main verb first form+ing+object

INTERROGATIVE SENTENCE

IS/am/are + subject + main verb first form+ing+ object

DOUBLE INTTERROGATIVE SENTENCE

WH family + is/am /are + subject + main verb first form + ing + object

PRESENT PERFECT TENSE
AFFIRMATIVE SENTENCE
Subject +has / have + main verb third form + object
NEGATIVE SENTENCE
Subject + has / have + not+ main verb third form + object
INTERROGATIVE SENTENCE
Has/have + subject+ main verb third form + object
DOUBLE INTERROGATIVE SENTENCE
WH Family + has /have + subject + main verb third form + object

PRESENT PERFECT CONTINUOUS TENSE
AFFIRMATIVE SENTENCE
Subject + has / have + been + main verb first form + ing + object + since/ for + time.
NEGATIVE SENTENCES
Subject + has/ have + not + been + main verb first form+ ing + object + since/ for + timing .
INTERROGATIVE SENTENCES
Has / have+ subject + been + main verb first form + ing + object + since/ for+ timing
DOUBLE INTERROGATIVE SENTENCES
WH family Has / have+ subject + been + main verb first form + ing + object + since/ for+ timing
PAST INDEFINITE TENSE
AFFIRMATIVE SENTENCE
Subject + main verb second form+ object
NEGATIVE SENTENCE
Subject + did+ not+ main verb first form + object
INTERROGATIVE SENTENCE
Did + subject+ main verb first form + object ?
DOUBLE INTERROGATIVE SENTENCE

WH family + Did + subject+ main verb first form + object ?

PAST CONTINUOUS TENSE

AFFIRMATIVE SENTENCE

Subject + was/were + main verb first form+ ing+ object

NEGATIVE SENTENCE

Subject+ was/were + not+ main verb first form +ing + object

INTERROGATIVE SENTENCE

Was /were + subject + main verb first form + ing + object

DOUBLE INTERROGATIVE SENTENCE

WH Family + was/ were + subject+ main verb first form + ing + object

PAST PERFECT TENSE

AFFIRMATIVE SENTENCE

Subject + had + main verb third form + object

NEGATIVE SENTENCE

subject +had + not + main verb third form + object

INTERROGATIVE SENTENCE

Had +subject + main verb third form + object

DOUBLE INTERROGATIVE SENTENCE

WH family + Had + subject + main verb third form+ object

PAST PERFECT CONTINUOUS TENSE

AFFIRMATIVE SENTENCE

Subject + had been + main verb first form + ing + object + since/ for + time.

NEGATIVE SENTENCE

Subject + had+ not + been + main verb first form+ ing + object + since/ for + timing

INTERROGATIVE SENTENCE

Had + subject + been + main verb first form + ing + object + since/ for+ timing

DOUBLE INTERROGATIVE SENTENCE

WH family + Had + subject + been + main verb first form + ing + object + since/ for+ timing

FUTURE INDEFINITE TENSE

AFFIRMATIVE SENTENCE

Subject + will/ shall + main verb first form + object

NEGATIVE SENTENCE

Subject + will / shall+ not + main verb first form + object

INTERROGATIVE SENTENCE

Will/ shall + subject +main verb first form + object ?

DOUBLE INTERROGATIVE SENTENCE

WH family + will / shall +subject +main verb first form + object

FUTURE CONTINUOUS TENSE

AFFIRMATIVE SENTENCE

Subject + shall / will +be + main verb first form + ing + object

NEGATIVE SENTENCE

Subject + shall / will + not +be + main verb first form + ing + object

INTERROGATIVE SENTENCE

Shall / will + subject +be + main verb first form + ing + object

DOUBLE INTERROGATIVE SENTENCE

WH Family Shall / will + subject +be + main verb first form + ing + object

FUTURE PERFECT TENSE

AFFIRMATIVE SENTENCE

Subject + will / shall + have + main verb third form +object.

NEGATIVE SENTENCE

Subject + will / shall + not + have + main verb third form + object

INTERROGATIVE SENTENCE

Will / shall + subject + have +main verb third form + object

DOUBLE INTERROGATIVE SENTENCE

WH Family + will / shall + subject + have + main verb third form + object

FUTURE PERFECT CONTINUOUS TENSE

AFFIRMATIVE SENTENCE

Subject + will / shall +have been + main verb first form + ing + object + since/ for + time.

NEGATIVE SENTENCE

Subject + will / shall+ not + have been + main verb first form+ ing + object + since/ for + timing .

INTERROGATIVE SENTENCE

Will / shall + subject + have been + main verb first form + ing + object + since/ for+ timing

DOUBLE INTERROGATIVE SENTENCE

WH family + will / shall + subject + have been + main verb first form + ing + object + since/ for+ time

References

- Tenses Anand Prakash Singh (2014) A complete handbook for TGT English 2nd Edition , Allahabad (Prayagraj)
- Tenses Dr. Surya Pal Yadav Trained Graduate Teacher Recruitment Test Agra .
- Parts of Tenses https://www.learngrammar.net/english-grammar/present-tense
- Parts of Tenses https://www.really-learn-english.com/english-tenses.html

Author Biography

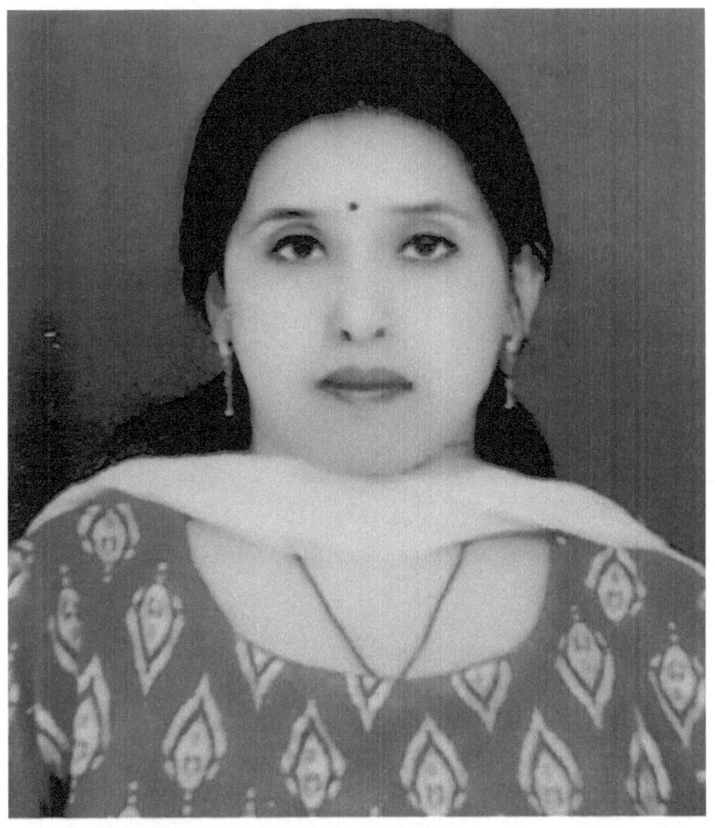

Ankita Singh

Ankita Singh is freelance writer. She has contributed articles in enormous national and international research paper and poems in various magazines. Till now her three books has been published in English and Hindi language.

She has done Masters in Journalism and Mass communication and M.Ed from University of Lucknow , M.A English and M.A Education from Dr Ram Manohar Lohia Avadh University uttar Pradesh . she has qualified UGC NET examination in Education .